# Sermons Will Ruin Your Life
A Collection of Poetry and Prose

Demitrius Burnett

No part of this publication may be reproduced in whole or in part, or stored in a retrieval system, or transmitted in any form or by any means electronic, mechanical, photocopying, recording, or otherwise, without written permission of the author. For information regarding permission, write to:

Demitrius Burnett
490 Lake Park Avenue, P.O. Box 16174
Oakland, CA 94610

ISBN 978-1-7343252-0-1 (Paperback)
ISBN 978-1-7343252-1-8 (Ebook)

**Copyright © 2019 by Demitrius Burnett**
*Sermons Will Ruin Your Life: A Collection of Poetry and Prose*
All rights reserved.
Printed in the U.S.A.

Photography: Behold, Creators
www.beholdcreators.com

To the Young Preacher,
or one in discernment, who needs to know
what you're getting into.

To the Seasoned Pastor,
who needs to see their experience
captured on the page.

To you, The Called,
you are not alone.


To my Wife, La'Vonnda,
Whose knowledge and wisdom have deepened
my understanding.

Thank you for loving me, for your patience, and for shepherding me through this book writing process.
I love you.

# TABLE OF CONTENTS

| | |
|---|---|
| Prodigal | 1 |
| Last Minute Prep | 4 |
| Longing for Tarshish (Jonah 4) | 6 |
| Joseph's Cell | 8 |
| Sleep | 10 |
| An Exercise on Breathing | 12 |
| The Dance | 13 |
| Family Time | 14 |
| Silence | 15 |
| … | 16 |
| What Happened to Us? | 18 |
| Shortness of Breath | 20 |
| Sermons…Will Ruin Your Life | 23 |
| 6 P's of Preparation | 25 |
| Consecration (The Holiest Part of the Week) | 27 |
| Sunday Morning | 28 |
| Taste of Victory | 30 |
| She Understands | 32 |
| Anamnesis | 35 |
| Confession | 38 |

*Sermons Will Ruin Your Life*

## Mark 8:34-35

### New King James Version (NKJV)

When He [Jesus] had called the people to Himself,
with His disciples also, He said to them,

"Whoever desires to come after Me, let [them] deny [themselves],
and take up [their] cross, and follow Me.
For whoever desires to save [their] life will lose it,
but whoever loses [their] life
for My sake and the Gospel's
will save it."

### The Message (MSG)

Calling the crowd to join His disciples, He [Jesus] said,

"Anyone who intends to come with Me has to let Me lead. You're not in the driver's seat; I am. Don't run from suffering; embrace it. Follow Me and I'll show you how. Self-help is no help at all. Self-sacrifice is the way, My way, to saving yourself, your true self."

# Prodigal

I've been — avoiding you
because I'm scared
of who you will become.
I'm scared of what it means for you to leave
this comfort zone
permanently.

I'm afraid
of the sacrifices it will take.
I'm afraid
of the decisions you will make.
I'm afraid
to see you climb too high because high climb mistakes
make falls great.
I fear what greatness means in *you*.

It's easy to be good — easy to be talented.
The gift in being gifted is coasting until gift is needed.
Then, you shine bright, are held up as great light
because it *look like*
you put so much preparation into your presentation.
It *look like* nobody work harder than you,
*look like* magic that can only come from you,
*look like* wonders from on high
that only come down to Earth in and through you.

But people don't know that what it *look like*…
ain't yo best you.

Because I'm *scared* of you.
Scared of the you, you 'sposed to be.
Scared of what this process is making of you.

*Greatness*…is. terrifying.

And "Normal" ain't part of your story's plot
*Twist*-ed formation of thought makes you think
the road to satisfaction goes through complacency.
Complainin', see, becomes a hobby as you witness yourself
not becoming who God made you to be.
Come plain and see the truth about you
you, livin' your greatest fear.
Come pain if need be to loose you – from *you*.
Come plane on sea of doubt, the great abyss,
Lift him above all this so he can plainly see

the Son, never stopped shining on me.

In *me* is still the Light I need to survive, to thrive,
set world aflame for the One who spoke through fire,

"I AM."

Reminding me of who He is,
"I AM THAT I AM."

The Holy One, Oh Ancient of Days,
"I AM."

The One who knew me, shaped and formed me
in my mother's womb before I ever saw sunlight's rays,

"I AM!"

And to, "That I Am,"
I am

Sorry.

I'm sorry
for avoiding You.

Loving You comes with more than an heir's benefits,
but also
Responsibility.
And it has been Irresponsible of me
to avoid You like this.
Irresponsible
to avoid the Person who made me,
avoiding my true self.

I'm. Sorry.

I repent.
I'm ready
to sit
and listen.

My heart is open
to Your Spirit.

# Last Minute Prep

Sermon,

You make me

                anxious.

Anxious
     about what you will make of me.
Anxious
           about what you will make in me.
Anxious
                about what you will make of yourself
and what I have to do with your development.

You make me
anxious in the kind of way that
causes me to ask myself,

*Why didn't I start this sooner?*

Makes me want to study,
but also embrace distraction,
do nothing instead.
Be amused with less important things
so I don't have to face your stare.

You make me — tired.

Barely gliding upon your sails,
drifting downstream,
floating upon shore and tracing your footsteps,
begging
to come upon their Source.

*God, can't I just finish this in the morning?*

Tired.

At tracks' end, I write you with my eyes closed,
sitting
rocking between sleep and prayer.

Praying and pushing,

*Lord, please help me finish this tonight.*
*Please help me make this…*
*Please help this make me…*

*Rite.*

# Longing for Tarshish
## *Jonah 4*

I'm not happy with You right now, God.

I didn't know being a called out one meant being called out of places I paid to be in. Moments with friends and family I've waited to experience present themselves and You steal them with instructions to go home. To go away from everyone I came, everyone I put miles and resources under foot to see, just to retire to my quarters – alone. In double minded faith that I'll actually experience a visit from my Master. In hopes of being trapped with You so it won't be an empty theft of time.

Until You arrive, my only company are these words. Words begotten by feelings. Feelings begotten by circumstances unpleasant. Circumstances unpleasant begotten by forces out of my control…I assume those forces were begotten by *You*… Immense wind and sun and once plush trees now withdrawn, all so You can get me alone in this empty, friendless, family forsaken – room.

To write what? This poem? A sermon? For people? You mean the people You just told me to leave? The loved ones this poem has stolen time from? You called me here to write something for them they'll only benefit from in the future when I could be with them in the now. This. Isolation by *Your* choice – is not where I want to be.

Caught between my heart's desire and obedience. Knowing I don't want to rebel because the cost is more than I may know. But, honestly, since I chose obedience, this cost – the absence of self from the realm of loved ones so rarely together – *this cost* is the only one I'm experiencing right now. And I can't even explain to them, can barely explain to myself — *why*.

This, is a moment I would have rather chosen disobedience. Chosen not to experience the sorrow of leaving as my heart begged to be taken back to Tarshish. Chosen my family. Instead, I have to be *here*. I have to retreat *here* and be with Someone I would have talked to about this when I got home. Work I already planned to do, *tomorrow*.

So, I'm mad at You – God.

I'm angry, and I'm hurt. I wasn't expecting this to be a night I'm called out of phileō into pain.

I missed out…for this.

# Joseph's Cell

somehow
this is the place i'm expected to produce
                                                    words
interpretation
                    "from God"
sleep
     weighs
like heavy legs on mile 25,
my mind - numb.
a gallery of static sound and screens
screams
too much deep thought today

what am i supposed to do in a place like this?

                          barren

trapped.
my study has become a decorated prison,
furnished with hardwood floors, walls of countless books,
the smell of old pages,
the aroma of fool's paradise
pervasive.

Night surrounds
but for rays seen under closed door.
that light

is my desperate hope…to leave this place.
it blesses and antagonizes me.
Night teases with rest as Light reminds me
sleep
                                    is yet a ways off.

there is light remaining
for the Work i must do,
this Holy Work which transforms
labor into fruit.
this Work which reminds me
it's not by my power, nor by my might.
this Work which calls me

to Spirit

to write by the substance of sermons hoped for,
the evidence of metaphors unseen.
to see beyond this page before me — an unfinished site
bring meaning to forgotten dreams.
make sure the people walk by what they believe,
not what they see

    *[sigh]*


        i dont need my eyes open to write anyway…

# Sleep

Hello Friend,

I appreciate you being there for me when Sermon and I are having a tough time. Sometimes, when you're so close to someone you need some time apart. To get some space, let your mind be in a different place. To rest from the heat of battle or passion of a dance. To sit back and take time to understand what they really said.

You help me do that when my mind gets too crowded with feelings, complex thoughts, and lists of things to do. Sleep, you help me get out the way when God is trying to speak something new, let revelation ease into me — Holy Spirit, imbue.

Let layers
       of pages
              and mind
                     unfold.

Closed eyes show me next steps, produce fresh words, give levity to weight from depth in Sermon's waters.

And I do love Sermon. I really do.
I understand it means well in its immersion ritual.
You just help me close my eyes so I can experience this baptism as spiritual, not momentary drowning.

You really are the best.

Thank you for letting me unwind
so I can willingly go
wherever Sermon leads me next.

Your Friend,

# An Exercise on Breathing

I stop breathing when I'm stressed.

I

Obstruct oxygen's flow *in*
Roadblock creativity's flow **out**
Bind my lungs *in* suspension
Race my heart **out** of normal pace

I

Hold my mind *in* tension
Trust my ability to figure it **out**
More than memory to draw Spirit *in*
Close eyes to block **out** distraction
Call ears *in*-to attention

Heaven's Radio

But almost **out** of range
Sig-nal -- fault-y --

*In*
                and **out**

*(Repeat as Needed)*

# The Dance

Back and forth we *sway*
through the night.
You close to me, me close to you.
Our places of creation almost touch.
In that "almost"
is the room we leave for Jesus.
Creative Presence exists there.

Just when the tension of intimacy gets too intense,
the next movement begins.
Suddenly more distance,
yet still connected at arm's length.

Distance helps me see you more holy.
Spin you, turn and reassess my position
as not to get in the way of your grace.
It is the distance that gives new perspective
and release from the tension.

Distance allows us to dive in
again
to this dance of proximity and breadth.
Ordered steps, together,
in rhythm of shoreline waves.
Illuminated by the light of Saturday's kairos.

# Family Time

Weekends don't belong to you anymore.

Time is measured and metered,
dispersed according to the rhythm of your "process."

Cycles of active and dormant,
communal and secret places.
Windows of being, "present."
Windows of your mind occupied
by Sunday.

Unsure about date night.
Can it be Friday or Monday - this week

Yours works in a different rhythm
that uncomfortably beats around you.
Syncopating itself to your offbeat
yearning for your rest.

To finally fill your sheet with notes
of laughter, stories of their day and week,
I love you's and everything
they've been waiting to tell you
while you were away.

# Silence

Be clear in my mind so I can hear.
Be clarity. Be sound.
I need to be sure the words are His.

Background of all thought, hold my thoughts.
Be fixture for Neural's connections to hang from
 ——lines suspending pictures which speak——
softly
and
slowly
as they develop in quiet, red rooms.

Images baptized in the Jordan - or Mississippi -
Hung high to dry.
Raised, not yet glorified – new image.
Touch it not until it is finished
developing under your care.

Be the film which Light shines through,
that it may project the message
until visible on the soul.

When impatient,
remind me of your mastery.
That I must step aside at times,
allow you
to do your work.

...

I've been trying to speak with You, God, for a week now…

and still no call back.

I pray and I pray.
I wait and I wait.
I have left You messages.
Stopped by Your House.
Sang to You.
Written whole messages to You.
And yet, You leave my prayers on

"read."

*...4:52pm 6/12*
*..2:07am 6/11*
*.9:01pm 6/10*
*7:06pm 6/10*
*12:47pm*
*11:08am*
*5:11am on the same DAY!*

YOU are the One who called me to this!
YOU are the One who wants me to preach!
YOU are the One who created whole worlds by *speaking*...

So why won't You speak to me?

Your silence is so *loud*...it hurts.
And I need to hear Your voice.
Speak to me, Lord.
Dad, please…

Speak.

## What Happened to Us?

I don't love you the way I used to.

I used to be excited about you.
couldn't wait to write you.
Would sit down in my free time, spend it with you.
Even wrote you on paper with pen
so I could feel you flow through my hand.

Now...
I'm sitting
writing poetry about my grief
of what we *used* to be.
The sad thing is, you haven't changed.
So that means, "It's not you, it's me."

I'm sorry.

I just don't feel the same.
So much within untethered.
Some disconnect that's keeping me from going
deeper.

I'm struggling to connect to our Source.

This once strong tree
was made hollow by the rot of disappointment.
It chewed through my armored self-esteem like bark
made of brittle perceptions of self in ministry
until it burrowed a home within the core of my being,

leaving me as raw resource —— exposed
to the relentless winds and waves
of ministry.

I just want, I just need
some time to be restored.
To heal.
To become an oak of righteousness again.

But God,
I'm not sure where to begin.

I just know I miss our conversations
that were just conversations,
and not about what You want me to say to Your people.
I miss garden sit downs and walks amongst bushes and trees
where we would check in about *us*,
when I could hear Your Voice
as if amplified through a speaker.

I miss singing to You
a new song You put in my heart
and I would write it down or record it,
even if no one ever heard it.

So, would You come sit with me, please?
Without the pressure of being Your speaker?
I may not know how to reconnect with Sermon right now,
but I know I need – You.

# Shortness of Breath

Sermon, why have you taken hold of my chest? Held under arrest my breath without Mirandizing, you haven't read a single right before clasping your cuffs…even tighter.

You, make a bed of my lungs. Tossing and turning throughout the night, wrapping bronchial lobes in the custody of your arms like snuggled favorite pillows. You squeeze harder like breathing exists to rock you to sleep, disregarding the fact that I need those to breathe.

You, Sermon, play tricks on my mind. Make Russian doll of yourself - veiling your presence *beneath* just being tired, *beneath* stress from so many deadlines, *beneath* guilt from spending too many hours in hobbies and pastimes, *beneath* emotional and mental fatigue, *beneath* layers upon layers until you're ready to be seen.

You nestled yourself in, put short leash on my breath and waited for me to be *still,* enough…to slow down, pray, open the Spine, remove all the layers, and open my eyes to see you.

Then, as I look at the Text — and remember today's news — I finally know what's been bothering you.

In all my confusion about our encounter, I realize I should've *known* it was *you*…

I should've known it was *you* disrupting my mood until you could settle yourself into the emotional cracks. I should've known you'd leave doubt, concern, a desire to discern, clarity and nothingness all at the same time until I stopped to open my eyes to why you've been crying.

I should've known it was *you!*
I should've known you've been watching the news.

Causing you to coil and writhe under my sternum like a large body resisting illegal chokeholds. Attempting to push your words up my throat like off duty cop through wrong apartment door. Except they can't get beyond the barricade of Adam's strange fruit. So all I keep getting is, "I can't *breathe.*" With this hold on me, I can't *speak.* And as I experience you, now I *see* why you had to do all this because now I *be* — the experience of the people.

*Years* of weary tears, and fear, and hopelessness, and faith, and marching, and faithfulness, and 911, and distrust, and caution tape, and flashing lights in blue, and white, and red and red and red and red and red and red
and dead.

Now, with noose 'round my neck,
the Nile and Middle Passage flowing through my eyes,
my heart laid bleeding 4 hours on Canfield Drive's concrete,

*I* am in *need* of *Resurrection!*

And here…still, small Voice whispers
to look at the pages again.

To pick up the pen. Write you, write about You,
a Moses message in the middle of the night…and
for the first time since you took hold of me, just…*breathe*

# Sermons…Will Ruin Your Life

Sermons are that needy person who wakes you up in the middle of the night because they aren't tired and just want to have some pillow talk. They are self-centered, and want your whole world to revolve around them — occupying all your brain space, emotions, and body as they nestle themselves into the tension of your muscles.

Sermons keep you in on Friday and Saturday nights writing, praying, crying, pleading, that God would just give that next word the people need to be free. The word that *YOU* need to be free from the burden, at least for the night. Nights – who am I kidding? Sermons take your whole Friday, Saturday, your week as they till your heart until it becomes good soil for them to plant themselves in and take root. Germinate. Fracture their shells until mystery is undone and Word pushes Its way through your soul toward the Light, springing forth on Sunday – harvest.

Sermons are deep water. They drown you in the depths of thought oceans so you can meet your Maker. So your pen can meet paper, so your fingertips can touch keys to keyboards that just want to lead you to Facebook and Netflix.

Sermons will fill you with poetry when you are supposed to be writing them.

Because they want to remind you Divine Spark is full of creativity. They will not be measured and metered out like they are a science. Sermon says, "I am ART...so act accordingly." And when you do, sermons will resurrect you from their waters with fresh Breath in your lungs and Living Water in your belly, full of vocabulary needed to tell it.

Sermons...*will* ruin your life.

But to have Life,
to share It,
sometimes
you just have to let them.

# 6 P's of Preparation

### Monday
*Rest. Allow yourself to recover from delivery. Spend time relaxing - alone, with family. Have some fun today and do what you want. Spend some time with God just to say, "Hey" and hang out. Turn the pages to find the text for the next Sunday. [Maybe.]*

### Tuesday
*Pray over that text. Read it and read it – read and pray again. Let it be confirmed and slowly begin to sink in. Today is for confirmation and images to begin. Don't forget your notes on immediate thoughts and revelation.*

### Wednesday
*Wake and pray some more. Worship. Read the text again. Let it speak to you throughout your day. Take notes as needed. Write on your lunch break. Read and pray again on your short breaks. You must begin writing tonight and putting form to your thoughts.*

### Thursday
*Let the Spirit guide your hands today. Write, type, text in cell phone notes – however you receive it, let it flow. This is not an intellectual exercise, but a spiritual discipline. Still, you will need your mind. Use your study and commentaries to show thyself approved – confirm what you see in the text is not imaginary. Then, write.*

**Friday**
*Give thanks for what you've received already. Pray that the path to connect thoughts and ideas is smooth. Let God's inspiration and your study meet and walk hand in hand on the road paved with composite of clarity, imagery, relevance and understanding. Take it for a test drive.*

**Saturday**
*Wake, pray, and worship. Give thanks and begin edits. Go for another test drive. This is the last day to get it in you and not just on paper. After your first run, spend time with your family. Trust it will find its way to your soul. When sundown arrives, retire to spend time with God and Sermon. You both need time in His Presence.*

**Sunday**
*Prepare body and mind. Shower, hot tea, praise and worship. Get dressed and make your way Home. Warm your vocal cords, carefully, in song and pleasant greetings. Step into pulpit…*

*It's time.*

# Consecration
## *The Holiest Part of the Week*

The holiest part of the week
is not Sunday.
It is not Sunday's morning light, which wakes
to prayer.
It is not in the worship selection
before preparing your voice.
It is not in that hymn.
It is not each step up those stairs to the pulpit.
The holiest moment
is in the time you take to go before Him.

(Young) Preacher,
to the seasoned and the wise,
never forget to fix your eyes on the preparation
before the presentation.
Never forget, your spirit's eyes need to see
before revelation is received.
Never forget, the holiest moment is not in
the Sunday morning loud and speaking.
It is in the quiet *quickening*.

# Sunday Morning

No alarms needed.
Sun's light wakes.
Son's Light waits,
stirs.
Begin to align mind, open eyes, dilate throat
with warm lemon tea and honey.
Inhale
Exhale
Sip and swallow.

We are here.
Pray the preparation is enough
as Sermon and I spend final morning moments together
before I must dress, prepare to leave home, and
enter the sanctuary.

We talk to each other during the ride as I rehearse
aloud, in mind,
and pray
that You, God will have Your way today.
Say what You want to say.

Fill in every space unwritten
that this holy union will be a threefold cord.
That Your Spirit would work in and through us
so that we aren't up there

Alone.

God,

Here we are
humbly accepting Your call
to be proclaimers of Your Word.
May every word, movement, and sound serve Your purpose,
point toward You and bring You glory.
Give us presence of mind to be present to Mind
throughout the service.
Help us lead, help us worship.
Center us now as we approach this holy pulpit
to proclaim Your Good News and Holy Work.
Let the words of our mouth and meditations of our heart be
pleasing unto You, Oh God.
We, as sanctuary, are Yours.

"Turn with me, if you would, to the book of..."

# Taste of Victory

Victory tastes like prime rib for Sunday Family Dinner.

Served hot, then dipped in relevance.
Smeared with measured cultural reference.
Next to mashed metaphors to stick to their ribs
so they don't lose their meal by the time they get home.
There's side salad tossed with storytelling, testimony, and
wit on word study mixed greens, dressed with eloquent,
yet digestible, cadence and verbosity.
Served on plates of biblical cultural context
and present-day criticism.

Victory tastes like the joy of your favorite ice cream.
Drizzled in caramel humility and chocolate gratitude that
you didn't embarrass yourself at dinner,
didn't dishonor your Father
by serving food undone
because you rushed through preparation.

It's sprinkled with pieces of candy-coated pride
because you improved in prep and plating,
checked every box to grow as a chef,
fed the people and honored your Father, your Dad,
the very essence of sweetness.
Achieving all your goals – the cherry on top.

As you hear the *mmh's* of your diners…
you get *full* off joy, and feel the *warmth*

of hearing your Father say the three words
you *have* to hear from Him
and *hope* to hear from your loved ones
after every. single. meal.

"You did good."

## She Understands

*To My Wife, La'Vonnda*

If you are going to love someone
who isn't God,
sermons, or poems,
they have to understand.

They have to understand
how your relationship will be between you,
God, and another.
They have to understand that you can't help the role Sermon
plays in your life. You can't help what Poem means to you.
The two are a part of you.
They cannot part no matter what you do.

Even when you die,
your sermons and poems will still speak
and keep them company.

They have to understand
that you probably didn't choose this.
That it chose you, therefore it chose them, too.
They have to understand that you need time alone,
especially on weekends.
*Especially* if adulting didn't allow you to prepare
like you wanted
sooner.

They may have to get used to, "I'm sorry."

They must understand that in loving you,
they are also loving the calling on you.
That they marry that, too.
Accompanied by all the dreams, visions, and metaphors
that will fill their ears with more words than they can handle.

Because they understand
you can be
fully the person you were called to be.
And they will be determined that
*that* person
is who you *will* be.

Because they're not sacrificing so much, making so much tea, waiting with you, holding you when the burden brings you to tears, breaks you, leaves them to take care of the household affairs then rock you to sleep; they are *not* doing all this understanding so you can live under-being.

So, they push you to do what you need to do,
be where you need to be.
So you, the people, and (prayerfully) the family
can be *free.*

They must understand.
You must value their understanding.

And, *you* understand *this*.

They are worth sermons being incomplete
if you are needed to help them stay whole.

They are worth staying when summoned to go
and *they* just need you *home* to silently hold.

They are worth saying, "No."
when their very presence merits your, "Yes."

They are worth more than your leftover energy,
they are worth your *best*.

So you plan for them, with them.
You manage your time when you know Sermon is coming.
Because Sermon is not meant to come between and separate
you and your loved one.

Even when alone with it,
it should help you love them
better.

And you *better!*

No matter the burden, no matter how duty calls,
*I* need to understand
that God has called *her* to be my first ministry.
That when I love God and her completely,
it allows me to do ministry – freely.

# Anamnesis

More than I need you,
you need me.
You need the quickening of my tongue,
giving rhythm and eloquence to your unsorted elements.
You need the rumble of my vocal cords,
vibrations giving voice to your words.
You need my feet
to position yourself behind pulpits
and speak to people's needs
that my eyes see.
You need these hands to be written, these lips to be given,
the contraction and dilation of these lungs
so you can keep living!

*You* need *me…*

> *To remember*
> *how this relationship works.*
> *Not only do you need me,*
> *but it's bigger than both of us!*
> *It's about our need of Him*
> *more than anything on this Earth.*
>
> *It's about how He started you from the*
> *bottom,*
> *molded and fashioned you from dirt,*
> *blew life into you,*
> *made you a soul,*

> *exhaled me into your nostrils,*
> *made us both alive*
> *and whole.*

Yeah, but you still need this dirt.
Without this clay lifted, shaped by Potter's Hand
you'd have no place to live,
no legs to stand.
You would be

> *Like the Son of Man?*
> *With nowhere to lay His head?*
> *See, without you, I'd still be like Jesus.*
> *But you? Hmm*

I would be *me*!
I would be *free*
to actually choose who I want to be
instead of who I *have* to be
to make wholesome accommodation for *you*.
This temple, could be whatever edifice I desire.
My desires – for once – could lead.

> *For once, huh? Mh.*
> *I... I don't know what I have to do*
> *to get you to remember...this is not about you.*
> *Not about the obstacle course you build for me*
> *as I run along the track of your mind.*
> *Not the strength in your stance,*
> *power of your projection,*
> *strengthened alignment of your spine.*

*Not about your intellectual capacity to grasp me
and eloquently proclaim the complexities of my life.
Not about the monetary value of our presentation,
the number of S's we collect with that vertical stripe.*

*It's about the One who
Hung
  so you would not die.
Spun this ball on finger
so joy would arrive
at passing of each night.*

*It's about the Living Water and Bread of Heaven
    come to end hunger and quench thirst.
It's about edifying His body and helping us
       be free from sin's curse!
It's about His Power
to transform Life and Death's worst!!!*

*I need you…*

I guess, I need…

**To remember where we both begin.
To lose ourselves following Him.
To stand ready and prepared for His next exhale,
so when He breathes on us again,
our souls can live.**

# Confession

As much as you torment me, Sermon, I love you. I feel alive with you. I feel so on purpose in our time together. These words, these rhymes and rhythms, they are only here because of the burden associated with loving you. They come from understanding the weight of what it means to be devoted to you, be called to you, experience my call through you.

These words are fruit of labor hung higher than I could ever grasp alone. Creatures of deeper waters than I could ever dive. So I write them, to ensure I don't drown. They are pockets of air in this underwater quest where you serve as guide to my Creator.

To be honest, I don't know what I would do without you. You have been with me since the days my zeal for God was fresh. You have been with me when I couldn't make life make sense. When I didn't understand how I could experience more grace than I've already been given, you, have been there.

There, you have humbled me, created hunger in me, made me fall deeper in love with the One who first loved me.

Thank you.

Because it was there, in the "process," that I came to love, thee.

# Author's Note

I write this letter to you, the reader, from the center of a labyrinth.[1] Though now at the center, the process of getting here has been much like sermon writing. In its nature, it is far from a linear process; yet, it guides your steps in the way you should go.

For me, my first step into the labyrinth of this book was when it was seeded, unknowingly, on the night of December 2, 2016. I was up to preach the next morning and dreading the experience of writing the whole sermon that day. The message was from Habakkuk 2:2 on vision and entitled, "Something to Run With." Amidst the anxiety that I now recognize and name as creative tension, I wrote the first poem, "Sermons...Can Ruin Your Life" on Facebook.

Ironically, in the creation of that piece, God was giving *me* "something to run with" as the first version of "Shortness of Breath" arrived a couple months later. Not long after, God would reveal the vision of this becoming a 20-poem collection. A collection that I am incredibly proud of and grateful to have you hold in hand today.

In your sermon writing – or creating and bringing into being what God has uniquely given you to provide for all of us – may this labyrinth of poetry and the process of sermonizing and creating also be your teachers. May you remember not to miss the gifts of the journey due to your eagerness to reach

---

[1] *Thank you to Rev. Dr. Liza Rankow and OneLife Institute for providing the space!*

the center – even the Center of God's Presence. There are gifts for us at each step and turn we take; a path that swings us closer and further from center so that we may admire and learn from all aspects of God's creation – including ourselves.

When you are far from Center and feel on the very fringes of God's Presence, know that you are still on the path. Know that there is a gift in pausing, looking around, reflecting, and honoring others with whom you cross paths. Walk with the faith that you will reach your destination. Know that though your journey to Center may be slow and long, it does not mean your walk is ever without Presence.

Be *encouraged* my Sister, my Brother, my Fellow Follower of Christ.

May God be with you each step of the way,

*Demitrius*

# Acknowledgements

I must first acknowledge that this book was God's idea. I wrote the first poem to release the anxiety of the daunting task. Thank You God for teaching me to search for You in the creative tension.

My wife, La'Vonnda Haynes-Burnett, has been my greatest teacher for this work. You have done *so much* to make this book and its release real. I can't thank you enough. I love you with all my heart. Though not published yet, her thesis for her MFA in Creative Writing (with an emphasis in poetry) was an inspiration. When the day comes that it is published, know that it was a great influence.

La'Vonnda, along with Dr. Raina J. León, served as my editors. Thank you both for the gifts of your time, encouragement, and deep expertise!

Raina, thank you for your review and for serving so graciously in both roles. Your perspective and guidance as a woman of faith, poet, professor, publisher, mother and friend allowed me to have the trust and receptivity necessary to make this book what God intended. You are a gift!

Thank you to Rev. Dr. Alvin C. Bernstine, for everything. You allowed me to put my creative learning into creative practice as a Youth Pastor. You taught me much of what I know about ministry and delivering sermons. You also had several meaningful conversations with me about how seemingly momentary assignments, and burdens, can become books. Thank you for lending your voice to mine.

Thank you to the legendary, Rev. Dr. J. Alfred Smith, Sr., my first preaching professor. It is an honor and a gift to be able to call you my teacher and mentor. I can't measure how much it means to me for you to review this work. An honor I almost feel unworthy to have.

I want to thank all my professors who allowed me to engage poetry in the academic context as a valid means of theological discourse. In particular, I give thanks for Dr. Christina Hutchins and her course, "On Beauty and Critique," where we engaged Beauty personified.

Through that course, and the opportunity to witness the regular, public ministry of my classmate and brother in the ministry of art and theology, Marvin K. White, I was exposed to the type of courage and writing necessary to engage God and Sermon in the way this book required. Thank you.

To all the pastors, teachers, and leaders over the years who have given me opportunities to speak, preach, and poet (yes, I made it a verb), thank you! You have all given me opportunities to grow into my voice and contributed to my growth as a man and minister.

To Bethlehem Missionary Baptist Church, you welcomed me with open arms. You loved me and made so much room for my gifts to flourish as I sought to do the same for young people. I am changed because of my time with you, especially you, YOB! Thank you.

Finally, to my parents, Jerrold (JC) and Faye Rucker, thank you for all you've invested in me. Thank you for always positioning me to have such an intimate relationship with Christ that He would call me to create this work. I love you. This is also fruit of your labor.

To all of you, my family, and more I could not name, thank you for helping me "become."

# About the Author

Demitrius Burnett is a worshiper, preacher, poet, and writer, who seeks to serve an Audience of One.

He moved to the Bay Area from Phoenix, Arizona in 2013 and is a native of South Side, Chicago. He is a Brown University graduate, where he played football while majoring in Business, Entrepreneurship, and Organizations. Demitrius is also an alum of Pacific School of Religion in Berkeley, CA. As a PSR Changemaker Fellow, he earned a Certificate of Theological Studies in 2014, and went on to earn a Master of Divinity in 2016.

Demitrius previously served as the Youth Pastor of Bethlehem Missionary Baptist Church in Richmond, CA for four years. There, he created the church's Hip-Hop worship experience, "Worship and Flow." Since, he has continued to bring more creative methods to worship and preaching throughout the Bay Area and beyond.

Currently, Demitrius works to address the affordable housing crisis in the Bay Area while helping non-profit organizations gain funding as a Program Officer at the San Francisco Foundation. As a minister, he continues to advance the Gospel through his preaching, poetry, and daily efforts towards building a just community.

*www.demitriusburnett.com*

Printed by BoD in Norderstedt, Germany